2/18

2/18

POETIC
PARENTING

BRIGHT BEGINNINGS TO FABULOUS FUTURES

FARRAH M. WALTERS

iUniverse®

POETIC PARENTING
BRIGHT BEGINNINGS TO FABULOUS FUTURES

iUniverse books may be ordered through booksellers or by contacting:

iUniverse
1663 Liberty Drive
Bloomington, IN 47403
www.iuniverse.com
1-800-Authors (1-800-288-4677)

Because of the dynamic nature of the Internet, any web addresses or links contained in this book may have changed since publication and may no longer be valid. The views expressed in this work are solely those of the author and do not necessarily reflect the views of the publisher, and the publisher hereby disclaims any responsibility for them.

Any people depicted in stock imagery provided by Thinkstock are models, and such images are being used for illustrative purposes only. Certain stock imagery © Thinkstock.

ISBN: 978-1-5320-2645-4 (sc)
ISBN: 978-1-5320-2646-1 (e)

Library of Congress Control Number: 2017909593

Print information available on the last page.

iUniverse rev. date: 06/26/2017

For Mike, Imagen, and Keenan,
the reasons for everything I do

CONTENTS

PREFACE

As I watch my children face harder decisions as they enter their teenage years, I can't help but think back to when they were much younger. I remember the guidelines and rules that my husband and I set, the lessons we tried to impart. And I hope that these lessons carry them through, bring them to a place where they can look in the mirror and like what they see and feel good about the people they are becoming. To me, that is the purpose of parenting: to create people that add to the goodness in this sometimes awful world, people who have that feeling inside that tells them they did their best and above all did what was right. I believe all of the moments when we tried to *show* them what was right, in addition to telling them, will matter in the long run. I hope when my children face difficult choices in life, they will look back and remember what they have been taught, and remember the triumphs, fun, and also mistakes that were part of the process. To be honest, my children have already surpassed what I could have hoped for their values and morals, and I am humbled to be a part of their continuing journey. I also hope that these stories are helpful to you, reader, and they can give you some direction in this most challenging path that we call parenting.

INTRODUCTION

As an educator and a parent, I have gained knowledge and experience with young people of all ages and ability levels, from diverse backgrounds. The completion of my undergraduate and graduate degrees in education has given me a foundation and knowledge of child and adolescent development, but it is the experience in the classroom, and the labor of love of raising my own children, where I have truly learned how to help young people develop into the best possible versions of themselves. Over the years, with others' children and with my own, I have seen similarities and patterns emerge. Every child, every person, needs to feel important and needs to feel heard. They need to know that they matter, but that everyone else matters, too. They need to be able to step into someone else's situation and to engage in how it feels, in order to become complete people themselves.

Good kids aren't born. They are made. It takes work, consistency, and a lot of patience. It also takes a healthy dose of humor and an acceptance of the fact that mistakes-lots and lots of mistakes-happen to all of us.

The idea to write a parenting book came to me slowly, as more and more people suggested it after meeting my kids and witnessing how they conducted themselves. I decided that the best way to impart the simple lessons contained here was through simple stories, in which siblings Emma and Ken reflect back on lessons from their younger days when facing tough decisions in their middle school years. These lessons involve their teachers, neighbors, friends, and some not-so-friendly classmates and peers. It is my goal that our experiences, fictionalized here in these pages, will provide enjoyable stories, which will then lead to teachable moments and conversation starters with your own children.

Lean close to your kids. Listen. Be proactive instead of reactive. Most of all, love them and make sure they know it, every day and no matter what.

POETIC
PARENTING

KINDNESS

"Emma, look at that kid. He's a loser."

As I turned to my friend Jessie, I caught sight of the boy she was talking about. It was pretty clear that he didn't fit in at Mountain Middle School, where I was a 7th grade honor student and aspiring spunky sport star. His clothes were different, and his behavior was strange. This was a kid in the small classes, a kid that came to school on the "short bus," the kind of kid that probably considered himself lucky if he was ignored rather than teased.

I knew I had a choice at this moment. I could ignore Jessie, I could join in the "fun" of teasing this kid, or I could stand up for him. That was a tricky situation because I didn't want to be known as "Little Miss Perfect," but the feeling in my stomach was telling me that being part of this was not who I am.

Suddenly, I was 3 years old, at a fast food restaurant with my mom and my younger brother Ken. Having just finished my kid's meal, I of course had to use the restroom. Give me a break-I was newly potty trained.

There were some people in the bathroom that, even at age 3, I knew were not "normal." They were flapping their hands and making strange noises instead of talking. My mom had promised me that she would always answer any questions I had about anything or anyone, as long as I didn't stare and I asked my questions later, when we were alone.

My mom greeted the people in the bathroom as she would greet anyone else, and back in the car, I asked my questions. My mom explained, "The people in the bathroom have autism. That's a disability that affects the way they act and socialize with other people." I learned a lot that day about people with mental and physical challenges. I know my mom dumbed it down for 3-year-old me, but I got the message: being considerate and nice to people who were different made the world a better place.

Back to the middle school hallway, and I knew what I had to do.

"Jessie, that's not cool. The kid has something wrong with him, and I'm sure he gets made fun of a lot."

I made sure that I said this quietly so I didn't hurt the boy's feelings. I didn't want to overdo the whole *be an upstander, not a bystander* thing, but I did go over to the kid and introduce myself. His name was Sam, and, it turned out, there was a lot that he wanted to share with me about his hobby of collecting trains. I listened for a few minutes, and I tried to ask questions that were related to his "train" of thought, pardon the pun. Then, I moved on with my day.

As a middle school kid, I wasn't out to change the whole world. But I could make my part of the world a little kinder with my choices.

When kids ask hard questions
Don't turn away
And think you will answer them
On some other day
Those moments are precious
Your answers will matter
To give them strength to be kind
When others will scatter

HEALTHY HABITS

"Ken, we're going to the donut shop. Do you want to come?"

As I considered Nate's offer, I remembered that I had track practice after school at Mountain Middle School, where I was a sixth grade science fiend and enthusiastic block builder. Honestly, it had been a tough day for a middle school kid. The math quiz was a killer, and I felt a headache coming on. I really didn't feel like running sprints today, and I knew some sugary donuts would give me a quick burst of energy to tackle my homework. I also knew from Health class that the energy would be followed by a crash, but I was still considering skipping track and heading to get those donuts.

Suddenly, I was 4 years old, and I was in the tiny playroom of the first house I ever lived in. My mom was jumping around, hair flying, sweat dripping, doing some kind of old-fashioned exercise video that involved kicking and punching. Of course, I wanted her attention back on me, so I told her that I was hungry. She smiled and said that she would get me and my sister Emma a snack after she finished exercising.

When Mom wrapped up her workout, she cut up a banana for us and added some peanut butter and fish crackers on top. In our house, this snack was the famous "nana bo-fish." Mom joined us with a banana of her own, and, as we were eating, she explained, "Fruit and exercise together help the body stay healthy so we can do fun things and think clearly for learning." Her words gave me something extra to chew on that afternoon.

Back to the locker room, and I knew what I had to do.

"Nate, I'm going to skip the donuts this time. I have to go to track practice." I went to track, ran my sprints, did my best, and felt pretty good after.

Later, after homework and dinner, I treated myself to some ice cream…after I had some "nana bo-fish," of course.

Treats and junk food
Are okay sometimes
And shouldn't be treated
As forbidden or as crimes
But on most occasions,
Exercise and good food
Are what keep us healthy
And in a good mood

CONFIDENCE

"Ken, how does it feel to be such a nerd?"

This was my classmate Albert, insulting me from across the table in art class. The teacher, Mr. Lorenzo, had just handed back our semester projects and complimented me aloud on my strong effort and attention to detail.

I didn't want to make a big deal out of this, and I really didn't want to look like a baby, tattling to my teacher. At the same time, I had that feeling in my stomach that told me that I didn't want anyone messing with me or talking down to me.

Suddenly, I was 3 years old, watching a battle scene in my favorite space movie with my dad in our basement. After a scene where the fiercest general obliterates an unlucky minor character, my dad paused the movie.

"You know," he said, "I always think of the general as giving his enemies the *death stare*." Of course, I had no clue what he was talking about and looked at him in confusion.

"I just mean that you don't have to argue or debate with someone who tries to mess with you. You can just look the person in the eyes, seriously and without smiling, and calmly say a few simple words. Then, without making a big thing of it, you show that person you can't be picked on and how you expect to be treated."

Later that night, I practiced my own death stare in the bathroom mirror.

Back to art class, and I knew what I had to do.

I looked Albert right in the eyes, without smiling, and I answered his question. "Actually, it feels good to be smart and know I'll be successful in the future. I'll probably also makes lots of money."

Then, I went back to my art project. That one was for Dad and the general.

Show kids it's important to be nice
But also to be tough
When people are rude
And the going gets rough
You can stand up for yourself
And do what is right
A stare and a few words
Show your strength without a fight

HONESTY

"Emma, I finally did it. I got that television app!"

My mom was excited, and I was too. I asked for the password, and my mom gave it to me on one condition: I had to check with her before watching anything that was rated for teenagers.

Fast-forward to that weekend, and my cousin Melanie was sleeping over. "Let's watch that new dystopia movie. I heard it's awesome," said Mel.

I knew that my mom would say that this was a movie she wanted to watch with me, in case there were inappropriate scenes I had questions about. Brutal.

But, on the other hand, I also knew that she trusted me enough not to check what we were watching, and that I could probably get away with watching it secretly. I considered my options.

Suddenly, I was 5 years old, at the mini-golf course that my brother Ken and I loved, a few towns over.

As my parents stepped up in line to pay for themselves and my little brother and me, my dad said, "Two adults, one four year old, and one five year old, please."

I noticed that the sign said the price was lower for kids 4 and under, and I had just turned 5 a few weeks ago. Would the half-asleep, pimply-faced teenager at the cash register even notice if my dad said I was 4?

After we walked away, I asked my dad why he didn't just pretend that I was still 4 to save some money. He looked right at me, and said, "Because honesty is more important than money."

Back to the sleepover, and I knew what I had to do.

"I know it's annoying, but I can't watch that without checking with my mom. She'll probably want to watch it with us if I tell her. Let's just watch one of our usual shows from the kids' channel."

We watched one of our old favorites, and it was pretty funny. I guess honesty is more important than money *and* movies.

If you are dishonest
You can't be surprised
If your kids grow up
And start telling lies
Show them through your actions
That honesty is best
And they'll do the right thing
When put to the test

BODY BOUNDARIES

"Emma, we're gonna play Truth or Dare. Let's dare someone to kiss Billy."

As I thought about what Allie was suggesting, I felt a little weird. We were in my friend Katie's basement at her birthday party on a Saturday night.

My friends and I had talked about boys, of course, and about the crazy changes going on in our bodies. But this was my first time at a party where boys were invited and people were talking about kissing.

I didn't want to be a goody-goody, but I wasn't sure I was ready for this.

Suddenly, I was 9 years old, and my mom was handing me a book and trying to talk with me about my "changing body." I was literally cringing and counting the seconds until the torture was over. My mom saw that I was dying on the inside, and said she would leave me alone with the book.

Before she left my room, though, she turned to me and said, "I know this is hard to talk about, but please always remember that you and your body are precious. No one in the world has the right to make you do anything that you are not comfortable with. You are in charge."

I was relieved when she left, but I did think a lot about her words, and, even though I never told her, I ended up reading that book from cover to cover.

Back to Katie's basement, and I knew what I had to do.

"You know what," I told Allie, "I think I'd rather save Truth or Dare for when it's just the girls. Maybe we can play Manhunt now that it's dark outside."

I knew that it would always be awkward to talk to my parents about that kind of stuff, but I would always remember that my mom was brave enough to "start the conversation" with me on an embarrassing topic. I would also never forget her main message: when it came to my body, I got to decide.

Our kids' bodies
Are precious indeed
And talking honestly early
Is what plants the seed
That they get to decide
What's right and what's wrong
When those tough choices
Surely come along

READING FOR FUN

"Come on, Ken, just one more level before you quit."

I told myself this as I played my favorite video game. I had finished my homework, and it was my relaxing downtime before dinner. I could feel myself getting frustrated and a little worn out from playing for so long, not to mention that my eyes felt itchy and tired.

I was thinking maybe I should switch it up and do something else for a little while, but I was tempted to keep trying to pass the level.

Suddenly, I was 3 years old, and my mom was reading to my sister Emma and me. After we finished the book, a funny one about our favorite bear family, my mom told us that books have always been a treasured part of her life.

She explained, "When I read a book, I feel like I'm transported to a different place. Movies and video games are great, but a book makes you work a little bit. You have to create the world, and then you get the privilege of being a part of it."

This was a little over my head at the time-Mom treated us like we could understand complicated ideas, even when we were little-but I guess I got the point. Reading was an awesome way to spend your free time.

Back to my room in late afternoon, and I knew what I had to do.

I picked up the book I was reading from the huge pile Mom had brought home from the library. Pretty soon, I was part of a fantasy world where dwarves and dragons wandered and battles were waged over shiny objects.

When Mom called me for dinner, I was shaken out of this new world, and I realized how hungry I was. I guess it made sense that I was starving, after all that "work" I did while reading.

Movies and video games
Are okay in a small amount
But reading is the best choice
To make leisure time count
Vocabulary, writing skills,
A new way for things to look
All of these can only be found
When you open a book

PREJUDICE

"Emma, did you hear that one of the teachers at the high school is gay? That's so gross!"

We were at the lunch table, and my friend Carrie was saying this just as I was about to bite into my lunch, a pb & j burrito with Mom's signature touch, a fruit leather layered in for good measure.

I had heard some of the rumors about the high school teachers. Apparently, Mr. Anton had bad breath, and Mrs. Jacobs liked to sing during science lessons. I was mostly wondering about how much homework they would give and if they would offer extra help like our middle school teachers did.

I had never really thought about the romantic relationships of adults, especially teachers, and I was stumped about how to reply.

Suddenly, I was 8 years old, standing near the kitchen counter where we always kept the daily newspaper. My mom was telling me to hurry up and put my shoes on, as she was getting my equipment and water set up for soccer practice.

But I just couldn't pull my attention away from a picture on the front page of the paper. It was a photo of two ladies kissing, dressed in wedding gowns.

"Mom," I asked, "what is this?"

My mom explained that our state had just made it legal for gay and lesbian couples to get married. I was speechless for a moment, and I stared at my mom for guidance on what to make of this.

She looked at me and said, "Em, people should have the right to do what makes them happy. There are many kinds of families. Who are we to judge what counts as true love?"

My mind was racing as I laced up my cleats that day.

Back to the middle school cafeteria, and I knew what I had to do.

"Carrie, I didn't hear that about the high school teacher, and I honestly don't care. It's gross to picture teachers kissing or holding hands with anyone. I don't need to think about who they do that stuff with."

We switched topics to our social studies project, and then the conversation moved on to our tournament game that coming weekend. It was not my place to judge people's private choices, and that's the way I liked it. I had enough going on in my own life.

Life is too short
To criticize others' choices
Everyone has a right
To speak out in their voices
When the moment comes
Seize on it; don't wait
Teach your kids tolerance
And never show them how to hate

DISCRIMINATION

"Yo, Ken, what's up, nigga?"

My friend Calvin was greeting me in the morning at lineup outside of Mountain Middle School. There were lots of kids around, of all shapes and sizes and colors, including some black classmates and friends.

This had become a common greeting at school, but I just felt weird about it. I debated if I should say something to Calvin or just let it go.

Suddenly, I was 6 years old, walking through the parking lot of a pizza restaurant with my dad, on our way to a baseball game. I saw a construction vehicle, which I know now is a backhoe, but which I used to call a digger.

"Look Dad!" I yelled, "It's a big digger!"

My dad looked uncomfortable and a little startled, and a bunch of customers were staring at us. I couldn't figure out what I did wrong.

Later, in the car, my dad explained to me that there were a lot of black people nearby when I said that, and he was worried that they might have thought I had yelled out the n-word.

He told me that the n-word had a long, horrible history for black people, including the time when they were forced to travel from Africa to America to work without getting paid.

Dad said, "This was called slavery, and it was one of the worst time periods in American history."

Back to morning line-up, and I knew what I had to do.

"Calvin, sorry, man, but I don't want you to call me that. That's kind of a messed-up word, and it's not cool to use it."

I didn't know if it made a difference, and I honestly didn't know if the black kids in school even cared that a lot of students used this word. But I figured that they knew the history of the word, like I did, and I thought that they probably were not cool with it.

Either way, I had to go with what I felt was right in this situation. I wasn't six years old anymore, and I knew that words had power, and that I was responsible for the words I used.

History is fact
And cannot be denied
We can teach kids lessons
Past mistakes have supplied
Show them equality and fairness
Have to come first
In this way we honor
Those who've been through the worst

EVERYONE MATTERS

"Emma, would you mind pairing up with Janie for the next project?"

My teacher Mrs. Fitzsimmons asked me this during 7th grade science class.

"Oh, no," I thought. I was hoping to work with one of my smart friends, because we could divide the work up more fairly and get a really good grade.

Janie was nice, but she was one of the kids who needed extra help. I knew that if I agreed to be partners with her, I would be signing up for a lot of extra work, and I would have to re-check and revise all of the parts that she did.

I looked up at my teacher, trying to make a decision.

Suddenly, I was 4 years old, having a play date at my house. There were a bunch of friends there, and I was trying to get everyone to listen to my idea for how to play school. All of my friends wanted to take a turn at being the teacher, but I was pouting and telling them that I got to be teacher every time because it was my house.

Suddenly, my friends got quiet and gazed over my shoulder. I could feel my mom's presence behind me, and I just knew she would want to weigh in on the topic.

She pulled me aside and said, "Em, it sounds like all your friends want to take a turn being teacher."

"But I want to do it *my* way, and that's what matters," I protested.

Mom got that look in her eye that said a lecture was coming. "Listen, Sweetie, sometimes you have to take one for the team and compromise. Always remember, you're the center of *our* world, but you're not the center of *the* world."

Back to science class, and I knew what I had to do.

I told Mrs. Fitzsimmons that I would be happy to work with Janie, and that I would make sure to help her out on the tricky parts of the project. As my teacher thanked me, I couldn't help rolling my eyes on the inside because I knew I would be in for a lot of extra work.

But it wasn't all about me, not all the time anyway. I could always choose a different partner for the next science project.

Our kids are important
And that they should know
But they also must learn
They're not always star of the show
Everyone matters
And all people count
Work with others, not against
To achieve and surmount

HELPING HANDS

"Ken, I know you enjoy the Environmental Club at school. Do you want to help out with the beach cleaning this weekend, even though you've fulfilled your service hours?"

Mr. Jones, my religious education teacher, asked me this question at class one Tuesday evening. We were required to do at least 20 service hours to prepare for our final sacrament of Confirmation, and I had just turned in my form with a sigh of relief at being done. Now Mr. J was asking me to do more hours out of the goodness of my heart.

I mean, I cared about the environment and everything, but hadn't I done enough good deeds for this year? I wasn't sure how to respond without sounding like a brat.

Suddenly, I was 7 years old, hanging out in the backyard throwing a football with my dad. Our neighbor at the time, Mr. Sanchez, was struggling to build a deck onto the back of his house.

My dad, who did construction work for extra money while he was in college, called over the fence, "Hey, Pablo, do you need a hand?"

Mr. Sanchez gratefully accepted, and Dad promised he would be over after we finished playing catch.

When we went to the shed to gather Dad's tools, I asked him why he was going to help Mr. Sanchez. I said, "Dad, you don't do construction anymore, and it's not like he was begging for your help."

My dad replied, "That's what neighbors do, Buddy. If we all help each other out, life becomes a lot nicer and a lot happier for everyone."

Back to Religion class, and I knew what I had to do.

I told Mr. J that I would help out with the beach cleaning, and I texted my dad to see if he would come along and help out, too.

Yes, there were other things that I wanted to do on the weekend, like seeing a movie and playing video games, but there was always time for those activities, too.

We were all kind of neighbors in this world, people and animals, and I could pitch in to make things a little better for everyone.

We are all so busy
With our responsibilities and roles
We can often get caught up
In personal matters and goals
But kids need to know
That helping others is key
To making the world better
For them, you, and me

TEMPER, TEMPER

"Emma, this can't be happening."

I thought this to myself as I stared furiously at the grade on top of my essay for Honors English. After all the work I put into this writing assignment, I felt that I deserved an A, or an A- at least. But a B- was totally unacceptable.

I was ready to march right up to my teacher, Mr. Collins, and give him a piece of my mind, but I didn't want to get in trouble. I was trying to get my temper under control, but, at that point, it wasn't happening.

Suddenly, I was 8 years old, in the car with my dad getting bagels on a Sunday morning. We always liked this time to talk and catch up on the week. We were right in the middle of discussing last week's recreation softball practice, which Dad coached each year.

Suddenly, a car appeared out of nowhere, cutting us off and forcing Dad to slam on the brakes. I could tell from Dad's face that he was furious. He didn't say anything. He just breathed deeply a few times and stayed quiet.

Later, he explained to me that it made him angry when people drove "like idiots" because it put the people he cared most about in danger. I knew he meant me, my little brother Ken, and my mom. He said he was sorry he got quiet, but he didn't want to curse or yell in front of me and set a bad example and possibly create a dangerous situation with the other driver. I could tell that it had been really hard for Dad to keep his temper.

Back to English class, and I knew what I had to do.

After a few deep breaths, I approached my English teacher. I explained that I had worked really hard on the essay, and that I would like to stay after class for a few minutes to talk about my grade. I didn't know if I would get the results I wanted, which included some writing tips and possibly a higher grade, but I knew that this approach was better than having a temper tantrum and getting a detention.

Turns out, Mr. Collins offered to stay after school with me, and he helped me improve the essay for more points on my grade. Score one for staying in control.

We have to show kids
That anger is okay
But losing your temper
Is not the best way
Stay calm and resolute
When things go wrong
This can lead to the outcome
You wanted all along

HANDS TO YOURSELF

"Hey, Ken, let me see that trading card you made."

My friend David yelled this across the hallway right after dismissal. I took out the card to show him, and for some strange reason, he threw the card on the ground and stepped on it. I knew that David was going through a rough time with his parents' divorce, but what the heck!

I clenched my fist, and I was really ready to punch him. I had to weigh my options here because I didn't want to get in trouble, and I knew that fighting was a one-way ticket to In-School Suspension. I thought about how to react.

Suddenly, I was 3 years old, and it was bedtime. I didn't want to go to sleep, so I was angry at my mom. At that moment, she leaned over to kiss me and tell me that she loved me. She reminded me sternly that I definitely needed my rest because my play-group holiday party was the next day. Mom had bought a special craft for me and my friends, and we were in charge of bringing my favorite holiday sugar cookies.

Suddenly, my frustration at having to go to bed and my excitement for the next day mixed together and built up, and I took a swing at Mom. She immediately held my hand right in front of her face where it had almost made contact. She looked me in the eyes and said, "We don't hit. It's mean, it's disrespectful, and it doesn't solve anything."

We didn't go to the holiday party the next day, and Mom made it clear that this punishment was a direct result of my attempt to hit her. She also made it clear that I would NOT be trying to hit anyone again, EVER.

Back to school dismissal, and I knew what I had to do.

I unclenched my fist and said angrily, "David, I don't know what that was about, but I'm really mad. That's gonna take me awhile to get over, so don't call or text me tonight or tomorrow."

I honestly didn't know if this was David's way of coping with his tough family situation, or if he was just being a jerk. Either way, I wanted him to know that what he did was not okay. Hitting wouldn't solve the problem, but I could show my anger with my words.

When rage builds up
As it does to us all
Tell kids to think
And make the right call
Think about your actions
When you're in a tough spot
Words can solve problems
And hitting cannot

SAFETY FIRST

"Emma, are you allowed on social media yet?"

My friend Amber asked me this question at track practice one day.

"No," I replied with a frown. "My parents gave me a whole lecture about how they trust me, but not the other people online. They even said that what I do online today could have consequences forever. I almost died of embarrassment."

Amber said, "You should try to convince them again. It's really fun seeing what everyone posts."

I thought about what she said, and I decided to give it another try with Mom and Dad. That night at dinner, I laid out my case, and my parents really seemed to be listening. In the end, though, the answer was still no.

"Sorry, Em," said Dad. "You just got your phone, and we think that is enough new responsibility for now. Our most important job as parents is to keep you safe. When you're in high school, we will revisit this."

That was not the answer I wanted, and I debated what to do.

Suddenly, I was 4 years old, and we were playing at the park with the other toddlers from "Mom's Club," a neighborhood group for stay-at-home moms and their kids. As always, Mom gave me the five-minute warning that it was almost time to leave. Regardless of the warning, I went nuclear when it was time to gather our things and head to the car because I didn't want to go home and take my nap.

As we got into the car, Mom had to struggle to buckle me in because

I was throwing my body weight around like a crazy person. Mom told me very sternly to stay buckled no matter how angry or frustrated I felt, because my seat belt would keep me safe.

As we pulled out of the parking lot, I decided to test the limits, and I unbuckled my seat belt while the car was moving.

We immediately pulled over and Mom told me, "When it comes to safety, the rules are non-negotiable. You will lose your video for a week, and you will NEVER unbuckle your seat belt again while the car is moving."

Since my brother Ken and I only got to watch one short cartoon video a day under Mom's strict screen time rules, losing this privilege was a really big deal. Needless to say, I was devastated. Mom stuck to her word, and I lost my video privilege for that whole week.

Back to the dinner table, and I knew what I had to do.

I said calmly, "I know how much you guys love me and want to keep me safe. I accept that the answer is no for now, but can we 'revisit' this in 6 months instead of waiting until high school?"

Mom and Dad agreed that this seemed fair. I didn't get exactly what I wanted, but sometimes you just have to take no for answer, at least for a little while, if it means being on the safe side.

When it comes to safety
No has to mean no
And it's not to be cruel
Or to put on a show
Kids have to realize
That their well-being and health
Are the very best forms
Of their family's wealth

STAY TRUE TO YOURSELF

"Ken, are you really wearing that shirt? My five-year-old brother has the same one."

I had my favorite t-shirt on, the one with the dinosaur video game character on the front, and my classmate Fred chose this moment in sixth-grade science class to make fun of my fashion choice.

I liked playing this funny video game, unlike a lot of my friends who played violent games that included killing and crimes. I wasn't allowed to play those games anyway, but honestly, I really didn't want to. I wasn't sure how to respond to Fred. Was my shirt babyish?

Suddenly, I was 3 years old, and my 4-year-old sister Emma was coming out of preschool, clearly upset about something and on the verge of tears. When we got home, she told my mom that her classmate Melissa was making fun of her hairstyle, which involved some kind of complicated braids on the sides of her head. Melissa said that it looked "weird."

Mom sat both of us down and explained to us that other people didn't get to decide what looked good on us. She said, "Em, you are beautiful no matter what, and I really hope you continue to wear your hair the way *you* like it."

The next morning, before school, my sister asked my mom for that same "weird" hairdo.

Back to science class, and I knew what I had to do.

"Fred," I said, "I really don't care what you think of my shirt or my choice of video games. I'm not a big fan of your sneakers, but I'm sure you're not going to run home and change them."

From there, we moved back to our science lesson.

The next day, when I was picking out my clothes, I chose another t-shirt with the same video game character on the front. That one was for you, Sis.

Our kids have to know
That they have final say
In how they express themselves
From day to day
Choices in style
May seem minor and small
But they provide free thinkers
With the chance to stand tall

THE GOLDEN RULE

"Emma, I know that I said I would come to your house after school, but I decided that I'm going to go over Jen's house instead."

This was my friend Ava, in math class one hot day near the end of the school year.

I was confused and asked, "Why? We've had these plans forever. We were going to paint our nails for the beginning of summer."

Ava explained that Jen's dad had just opened their pool, and they were planning to go swimming.

"We can do our nails any time," she said casually.

I didn't want to make her feel bad, but I knew that I wouldn't blow her off for another friend. I debated how to respond.

Suddenly, I was 8 years old, and my dad and I were playing basketball in my grandparents' driveway.

Some of my cousins, my brother Ken, and the neighborhood kids were playing with us. One of the kids from my grandparents' street started trash talking to one of my cousins about his basketball skills, or lack thereof, and I could tell that my cousin was about to either cry or insult him back.

Dad stopped the game and gathered the kids around. "Listen," he explained, "there's one rule I always follow when it comes to the way I treat other people. It's called the Golden Rule, and it means that you treat others the way you want them to treat you. No one likes being made fun of, so don't make fun of other people."

Without directly calling the kid out, Dad found a way to give all of us a lesson in how to treat other people. After that, the game went on much more smoothly.

Back to math class, and I knew what I had to do.

"Listen, Ava," I said, "I don't want to make a big deal out of this, but it's not fair to cancel plans at the last minute. I wouldn't do that to you. In fact, I turned down plans with my neighbor because I knew we were hanging out today."

Ava admitted that she had been unfair and suggested that we all get together so that no one was left out.

"I think that's a great idea," I said. Thanks for that one, Dad.

When kids are deciding
How to treat others
The Golden Rule has to be explained
By their fathers and mothers
Treating others as yourself
Shows ethics and smarts
And saves all of us
From broken feelings and hearts

Printed in the United States
By Bookmasters